★ NANA'S A STORYTELLER ★

THE MAGIC MIRROR

ANNE MARIE GODIN

ILLUSTRATED BY A. SIMIONI

The Magic Mirror

Copyright @ 2021
Anne Marie Godin

Illustrated by A. Simioni

YGTMedia Co. Press
Trade Paperback Edition

Published in Canada, for Global Distribution by YGTMedia Co.

www.ygtmedia.co/publishing

ISBN 978-1-989716-46-5

All Rights Reserved. No part of this book can be scanned, distributed, or copied without permission. This book or any portion thereof may not be reproduced or used in any manner whatsoever without the express written permission of the publisher at publishing@ygtmedia.co —except for the use of brief quotations in a book review.

Printed in North America

DEDICATED TO:

Nash, my joy, may you always remember how unconditionally loved you are.

This is how it always is: you open a book and the dedication is not for you.

Not this time.

All those individuals who are missing someone in their life, this is to you.

There are many more chapters to unfold in life and much more unconditional love to embrace.

Love You to the Moon and Back!

Not too long ago,
the WORLD seemed so small.
Now we're all so "CONNECTED,"
yet can't go outside at all.

Nana was trying really hard to keep **VERY BUSY.**

She needed to stop her mind from going into a TIZZY.

Nana tried
DANCING,
   KNITTING, and
PAINTING too.

She MISSED all the children though, this just wouldn't do.

NANA needed to see them and wanted to say,

"I miss you and your HUGS, come over to play."

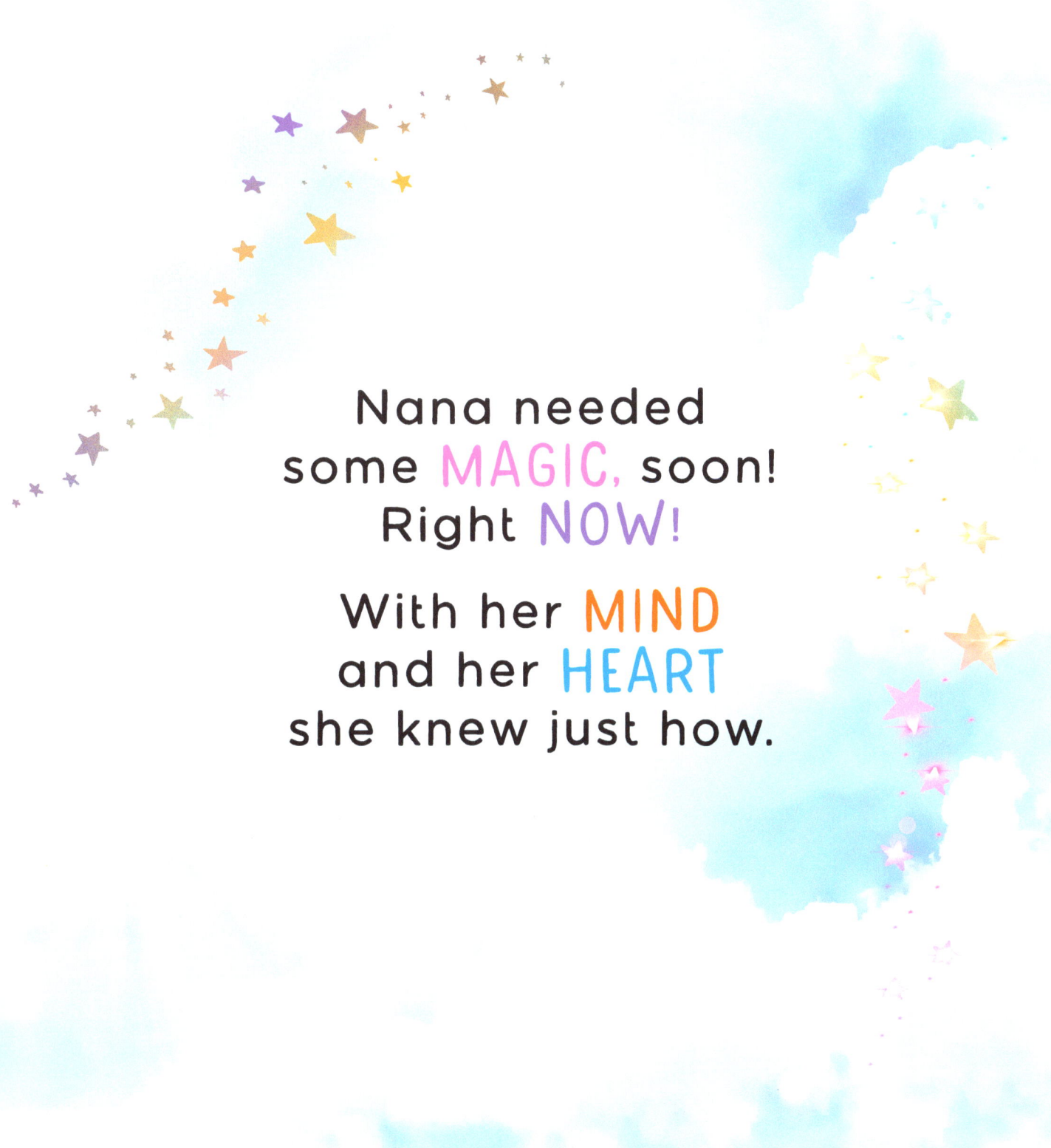

Nana needed some MAGIC, soon! Right NOW!

With her MIND and her HEART she knew just how.

Nana's HEART went pitter-patter as it gave her the feels. Ruby and Alfie RAN quickly, right at her heels.

Nana went to the shed to **SEARCH** through the bins.

She grabbed Nash's old BLANKIE,

Mack's **STRING,**

and Ford's TINS.

Nana found Harlow's HAMMER

and Thea's
SPARKLES
in blue.

She borrowed Hayley's PAINT

and Clive's **CRAYONS** too.

She grabbed Jaxon's
JUMP ROPE

and Malakai's BALL,

With Nathan's old BIKE BELL, she now had it all.

Last but not least, there was Tobi and Theodore's GLUE.

She thought to herself,
"I will make

MAGICAL MAGIC.

Yes, this will do."

1. MALAKAI'S BALL FLATTENED

2. FORD'S COOKIE TIN LID

3. ATTATCH BOTH WITH MACK'S STR...

4. CUT HANDLES FROM JAXON'S JUMP ROPE

(HANDLE)

8. COLOUR SPARKLES

Nana got straight to work with her RULER and PAPER.

She would craft up a magical mirror, like a MAGICAL MAKER.

Nana put on her GLASSES,
like when playing I Spy.

She HAMMERED and GLUED,
till the stars filled the SKY.

She held her magic mirror in the light of the MOON.

Then WISHED with all her might,

she would see the CHILDREN soon.

"I SEE Nash and Harlow,
Mack, Ford, and Clive too!
Oh my, there's Jaxon,
Malakai, and big brother
Nathan TOO!
There's Tobi, Theodore,
Thea, and Hayley.
Woo-Hoo!"

The children were HAPPY,
as she knew they would be.

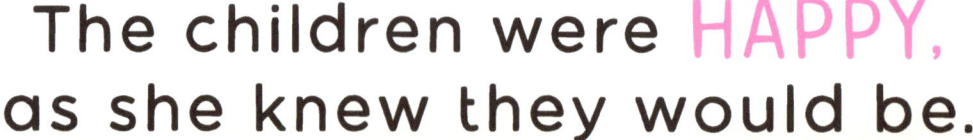

They all LAUGHED with great JOY,
their hearts filled with GLEE.

Nana couldn't give hugs. MAGIC and blowing KISSES must do. Forever and always, Nana sends "I LOVE You."

★ BIO ★

ANNE MARIE GODIN—CANADIAN AUTHOR, CERTIFIED COACH PRACTITIONER, DNA-GENEALOGY SPECIALIST, PUBLISHED PHOTOGRAPHER, RETIRED WEALTH ADVISOR

Anne Marie is passionate about how our mindset affects our ability to navigate life throughout our journey. She enjoyed nearly two decades as a private wealth advisor and mentor. A prolific writer and photographer, she has published in both mediums throughout Canada.

She is the author of *The Magic Mirror*, a children's book, and *The Long Hauler*, a nonfiction novel. She has been featured on several podcasts and has contributed and supported health advocacy, women, children, and Indigenous programs.

She is a lover of the arts and sciences, is a voracious reader, and is a blues and jazz enthusiast. Anne Marie volunteers her time as a DNA-Genealogy specialist for Bio-tracing. She is an animal lover and is passionate about health, yoga, meditation, and breath work.

Anne Marie was born in Toronto and raised in Willowdale, Ontario. She lives with her husband and their beloved yorkies in the beautiful Muskokas. She is the mother of three grown sons and is a nana.

www.ingramcontent.com/pod-product-compliance
Lightning Source LLC
Chambersburg PA
CBHW041059070526
44579CB00002B/13